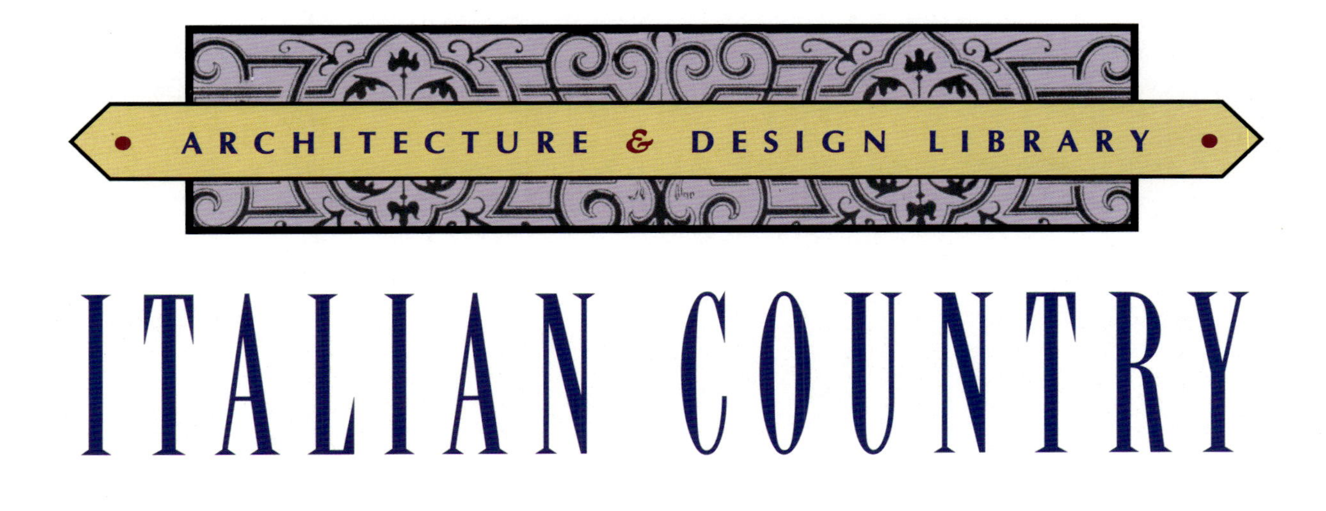
ARCHITECTURE & DESIGN LIBRARY
ITALIAN COUNTRY

# ITALIAN COUNTRY

*Robert Fitzgerald*

**A FRIEDMAN/FAIRFAX BOOK**



Library of Congress Cataloging-in-Publication Data

Fitzgerald, Robert, date
Italian country / Robert Fitzgerald.
p. cm. -- (Architecture & design library ; 3)
Includes index.
ISBN 1-56799-364-8
1. Decoration and ornament, Rustic--Italy. 2. Interior decoration--Italy. I. Title. II. Series: Architecture and design library ; 3.
NK2052.A1F58 1997
747.25--dc20 96-28411

Editor: Francine Hornberger
Art Director: Lynne Yeamans
Layout Design: Robbi Firestone
Photography Editor: Wendy Missan
Production Manager: Camille Lee

Color separations by Bright Arts Graphics (S) Pte Ltd.
Printed in Hong Kong by Midas Printing Limited

10 9 8 7 6 5 4 3 2 1

For bulk purchases and special sales, please contact:
Friedman/Fairfax Publishers
Attention: Sales Department
15 West 26th Street
New York, New York 10010
212/685-6610 FAX 212/685-1307

Visit our website:
http://www.metrobooks.com

*To my parents for their love and support.*

# *Contents*

# INTRODUCTION

P*iu se spenne e pejo se magna.* A curious expression, although one heard frequently in homes, markets, and local trattorias throughout the Italian countryside. Literally the proverb says, "The more one pays, the worse one eats," although the spirit of the words is lost in translation. In Italy, where hours are often spent luxuriating *a tavola*, or at the table, culinary rhapsody often inspires proverbial wisdom. The food that nourishes these ideas is remarkably uncomplicated, made from fresh, natural ingredients prepared in a simple way. What could be more delicious or easier to make than *un sugo di pomodoro*, a pasta sauce made with olive oil, garlic, ripe tomatoes, and a few sprigs of fresh basil? Italian country life is just as sweet and simple. The proverb, in fact, celebrates this lifestyle as much as it warns against the pitfalls of more indulgent cuisine. Long and languorous afternoons spent dining alfresco—in the dappled shade of a pergola overlooking the Italian countryside, perhaps—aptly demonstrate the wisdom of the words.

The Italian *campagna*, or countryside, stretches the length of the peninsula, from the northern Alps to the southern coasts of the Mediterranean, but it is the natural beauty of the central peninsula that conjures the most vivid images of Italian country life. The landscape, rustic architecture, and simple lifestyle of this region have come to define true Italian country living for most Italians and Italophiles alike.

The landscape of central Italy is marked by gentle umber hills and majestic cypresses feathering the sky. Roads twist along sheep pastures and broad meadows, and olive trees shimmer in the sun. One cannot fail to notice the quality and variety of light as the sun moves across the sky, continually altering the palette of this rugged terrain.

Nestled along peaks and valleys, far removed from roadways, sit quaint farmhouses—*case coloniche*—which appear as natural in this landscape as the vineyards and copper fields over which they preside. These farmhouses are typically built like small fortresses. Walls are constructed of creamy beige stone and roofs are covered with *coppi*, curved terra-cotta tiles. From the outside these houses appear squat and strong, classically proportioned. They are large but self-contained and rarely have more than two floors.

OPPOSITE: *Vineyards abound throughout Tuscany. During the* vendemmia, *or grape harvest, friends, family, and neighbors pick grapes at a feverish pace while the fruit is perfectly ripe. Three years later, the wine is ready for toasting.*

These farmsteads are simple and unpretentious, having originally been the exclusive domain of *contadini*, the tenant farmers who worked the land under the *mezzadria* sharecropping system. After the system was abolished in the 1950s, farm laborers left the country to seek better wages in the cities. In many cases, farmhouses that had been in families for generations were abandoned. In recent decades, as the modern world has become increasingly hectic, a new appreciation has emerged for these dilapidated old farmhouses, which are bought and converted into splendid country retreats. Medieval towers and small castles, relics from the age of warring city-states, as well as abbeys, monasteries, and grand villas are also real estate prime for renovation. It is the simple farmhouse, however, so elegant in its design and modest in its means, that embodies the essence of Italian country life.

For visitors from all over the world, the charm of the Italian countryside has proved irresistible. The British were the first to arrive, buying up properties in Tuscany early in the twentieth century. The Italians themselves were slow to follow and only in recent years began buying country houses in large numbers.

Converting farmhouses is not as simple as throwing on a few coats of paint. Often farmsteads are not equipped with running water or proper sanitation. Electrical wiring can be scary at best. Farm tenants lived in quarters upstairs, which were reached by external wooden staircases. Quite a bit of remodeling is often necessary as well, because the ground floors of most *case coloniche* were originally constructed as animal stables. The ground floor is commonly converted into a kitchen and living area, and the vaulted brick ceilings are, in some instances, painted white. Internal staircases must be added, and if the house is to be used during the winter, a heating system will likely have to be installed. All in all, renovating is no small task. Nevertheless, city dwellers still flock to the country undeterred.

Renovated interiors are spacious and comfortable. Furnishings are few and include only finely made, modestly designed pieces. To maintain a sense of rustic authenticity, rooms remain largely undecorated. Walls and floors are left bare, ceiling beams exposed. The spare symmetry of the decor and the simplicity of the furnishings emphasize the strength and boldness of the architecture. The natural elements come together in a concert of texture and color. Smooth surfaces play against rough, warm tones against cool.

The austere design of Italian country houses reflects the ruggedness of the surrounding landscape. It is this earthbound quality that makes life in the Italian countryside so enchanting. In every aspect, country retreats suggest a life far removed from the stress and strain of the modern world. The rustic nature of *le case coloniche*—like the uncomplicated goodness of the local cuisine—characterizes a refreshing way of life, one that embraces simple pleasures and is in many ways uniquely Italian. *La dolce vita* indeed.

OPPOSITE: *This living room's tall, vaulted brick ceiling serves as a reminder that the space once functioned as an animal stall. The room is now spacious and elegant, with a chair and sofa covered in simple white cotton, a time-honored country standard. The floors have an earthy, matte finish that visually softens the decor. Hanging baskets filled with dried herbs and flowers are a nice rustic touch.*

LEFT: *Hanging from ceiling beams or displayed on countertops, cooking utensils can bring fascinating geometry to the kitchen. A good heavy mortar and pestle is a wonderfully simple implement—a remarkable synthesis of form and function. A hanging bread stand is perhaps more whimsical, but nevertheless interesting to look at. Wooden spoons and ladles are usually kept in jars beside the stove to ensure easy access during frequent cooking frenzies.*

RIGHT: *In this Italian country–style bedroom, little can be done to enhance the majestic vaulted octagon ceiling. Such a setting requires only bare white walls and a polished wood floor to make it a place of beauty.*

PBC
1847

CHAPTER ONE

# ARCHITECTURAL DETAILS

The beauty of *la casa colonica* lies in the integrity of its building materials and the solidity of its construction. The Italian farmhouse is very much a sum of its parts, and in most cases the parts haven't changed for generations. From the *colombaia*, or dovecote, at the crown of the roof to the rosy *cotto* floor, the country house appears almost the same today as it did a century ago. That, of course, is the lure of the Italian countryside. The sense of timelessness is what fascinates.

Building materials are as old as the land itself and, in many cases, pulled right from the earth. Wood and stone form the foundation of all country houses, and even manmade elements such as stucco and terra-cotta, which translates literally as "cooked earth," reflect their natural origins. The combination of these materials, with their warm colors and rich textures, gives *la casa colonica* its rustic elegance.

The walls of Italian farmhouses are fortress-thick, sometimes more than two feet (46cm) wide to protect against heat and cold. They are built with local stones that are joined with lime mortar. Inside walls are generally left bare or are covered with a coarse, rich layer of stucco. Stone walls can also be painted with pink- or sepia-toned earth dyes, which lend the stones and mortar a mellow glow. In any case, the texture of the walls suggests the integrity of their construction. Nothing is hidden here, and the simplicity of form and function is refreshing. Not surprisingly, very few paintings hang on the walls. If a painting is put up, it usually commands an entire wall.

The rough texture of the walls plays well against the smooth surfaces of the terra-cotta floors. Red *cotto* bricks and tiles are often used to cover every floor in the house, although hardwood floors are not uncommon. Terra-cotta tiles are usually rectangular, a shape well-suited for intricate herringbone designs. Generally the floors are polished and waxed to a high gloss, although a weathered, matte finish can be effective as well. The older the tiles get, the more serene and impressionistic they become. Time and traffic smooth the tiles and give them a soft quality. Rooms are never carpeted wall-to-wall, although oriental rugs, kilims, or sisal rugs are occasionally used to accentuate the warm hues of the terra-cotta.

OPPOSITE: *Solid masonry is the foundation of every Italian countryside villa or farmhouse. Shutters help insulate the house from intense summer heat. Curved terra-cotta tiles known as* coppi *cover roofs and entryways. Nature is an integral design component: ivy slithers up walls, while wisteria creeps along the pergola and the second-floor loggia.*

Massive and splendid wooden beams support the ceilings of most farmhouses. Hand-sawn and roughly striated, these beams are usually made of oak or chestnut and given a glossy coat of wax. On these large beams rest smaller, perpendicular wooden joists, which in turn support thin bricks called *pianelle*, the base for the floor tiles above. This complex network of beams and joists creates a visually interesting space. Leaving these heavy beams exposed brings a sense of musculature to the room. In some rooms—bedrooms especially—the ceilings are whitewashed to lessen their severity and create a more intimate setting.

To aid in insulating the house, windows are traditionally small and deep-set, adding to the building's staunch disposition. Inside and out, louvered shutters are used to protect against the beating sun. Curtains were not traditionally hung, although in recent times sheer, elegant drapes have been employed to soften the effect of bare windows. With or without curtains, the shutters remain. Outside they are stained dark brown or painted in verdant or ocher hues; inside they are commonly painted white.

In keeping with the castlelike construction of the house, external doors are often quite imposing. Doorways, like windows, are distinguished by travertine or *pietra serena* lintels set in the walls. Heavy wooden front doors are decorated with bolts, hinges, and other ironmongery that would have traditionally been made by the local blacksmith. In renovated farmhouses, more delicate French doors have been installed in the archways where cowshed doors once hung, opening onto sprawling terraces.

ABOVE: *Fine craftsmanship is the hallmark of Italian country design. These graceful French doors lead from living room to terrace in a renovated farmhouse. Ironically, animals once passed through this archway as they came and went from their stalls. The farmhouse conversion was impeccable, however, and the result is a typically simple, elegant Italian domain.*

RIGHT: *Although running water is now enjoyed throughout Italy, a private well was considered a luxury not so long ago. This renovated seventeenth-century villa has kept its carved marble font as a picturesque memento of the past. The wrought-iron wellhead, window grates, and carved masonry attest to the skill of generations of local craftsmen.*

LEFT: *Ruddy salmon is perhaps the color most emblematic of Italian dwellings. Warm and subtle, this reddish-orange hue changes with the passage of the day and is deliciously evocative of the scorching Mediterranean sun. This ubiquitous tint actually looks better with age and seems to take on an entirely new countenance over the years. Here, tendrils of dark green ivy climb the walls, creating a vivid contrast of hot and cold colors.*

**RIGHT:** *Reflecting the influence of countless Mediterranean cultures over the centuries, Italy's southern landscape features some of the country's most unique architecture. Hundreds of years old, the domed houses of Alberobello are a perfect example. To insulate against the scorching heat, walls are several feet thick and vaulted roofs are stacked high with terra-cotta bricks.*

**BELOW:** *A bird's-eye view of a hillside town reveals an intricate patchwork of tiled rooftops resembling a cubist collage. Curved terra-cotta roof tiles are prevalent throughout the Mediterranean, yet each region has a distinctive hue. Terra cotta is—simply translated—cooked earth, so the color and texture of the local soil are directly reflected in the architecture.*

**ABOVE:** *Villa architecture is simple and elegant, marked by low-arched tile roofs with wide eaves and either stone or stucco walls. Decoration is spare but refined, limited to molded lintels above doors and windows and slender, wrought-iron balustrades along balconies.*

**LEFT:** *In northern Italy, the influence of Gothic architecture is apparent in many of the older country villas. The carved stone balcony of this former monastery opens onto a courtyard. Doors and windows are accented with both trefoil and pointed lancet arches, as well as decorative spiral columns. Picturesque decay enhances the exterior walls, where layers of stucco have deteriorated to reveal the original red brick.*

ABOVE: *Roadside trattorias and taverns in the countryside are rather inconspicuous, sometimes marked by little more than a small painted sign. The decor is typically quite spare, although a bombastic wrought-iron* gallo, *or rooster, typifies the lighthearted spirit of many country artisans.*

RIGHT: *The forest regions to the north feature some of the most intriguing architecture in the Italian countryside. Here, a nineteenth-century house literally merges with nature. Ivy climbing the walls lends an aspect of fantasy and evokes a mysterious charm.*

**ABOVE:** *This renovated* casa colonica *is a paragon of Italian country style. All the building materials reflect the colors and textures of the surrounding landscape, from the* pietra serena *stone walls to the terra-cotta* colombaia, *or dovecote, on the roof. The design of the house is modest yet well proportioned, a study in simple elegance.*

**RIGHT:** *Modern country houses adhere to the same aesthetic principles of more antiquated retreats. Here, the interplay of contrasting colors and textures is remarkable. Salmon-colored stucco walls are infused with strands of lush green ivy. Black shutters accent white windows and intensify the rich verdant hues of the lawn and vine-covered pergola. Even the terra-cotta planters in the garden complement the* coppi *roof tiles.*

**LEFT:** *Along the Amalfi Coast, buildings are often whitewashed inside and out. This pergola has classical plaster columns and a bamboo trellis roof. Pristine white curtains further protect the terrace from the sweltering sun and look quite elegant as well. Blue seat cushions give off a cool glow.*

**RIGHT:** *On the island of Capri, many terraces are white-washed and trimmed with glazed ceramic tiles. Often these handmade tiles tell a story—historical or legendary—that relates to the island. Here, the tile work—an artist's vision of what the harbor may have looked like a century or so ago—seems to mirror the scene below it.*

ABOVE: *Here, an oasis of lush foliage seems to transform the piazza into a tranquil country getaway. The small towns dotting the Italian countryside do, in fact, feel quite removed from the pressures of the modern world, and offer great weekend escapes from life in the city.*

**LEFT:** *Statuary is found not only on manicured estates, but also in the more modest gardens of the average* casa colonica. *A phalanx of Renaissance statues lends an air of antiquity to a grove of potted lemon trees in this charming garden.*

**BELOW:** *Typically overgrown by ivy, statues nestled in shrubbery or otherwise absorbed by nature imbue outdoor spaces with a sense of antiquity. Stone* putti, *or cherubs, enliven many Italian gardens.*

**OPPOSITE, TOP:** *Sheltered within the medieval town walls of Lucca, the sprawling Villa Torreggiani features a host of classical garden follies and statuary. The impressive staircase leads from a radiant flower garden to a broad, majestic fountain lined with sculptures.*

**BELOW:** *Italy boasts some of the world's most opulent country estates, and Villa Maser is certainly one of the grandest of all. In the gardens, a baroque, nineteenth-century temple folly is decorated with a pantheon of reveling Dionysian nymphs and cherubs.*

ABOVE: *Located on the slopes of the Dolomites, this rustic chalet is indicative of many houses in the region. Small windows help insulate against cold in the winter, while high-pitched gables keep snow from piling up on the roof. Similarly, long eaves protect the entrances and walkways from heavy snowfalls. Rough-hewn wood beams and walls made from local blond stone integrate the house into its natural surrounding.*

ABOVE: *The canals of Treviso wind along lovely homes as well as several charming old factories. This brick textile mill dates from the early twentieth century. With eaves rising and falling and colorful bands of paint lining the walls, the building itself makes an interesting weave.*

acqua
REX

CHAPTER TWO

# KITCHENS AND DINING ROOMS

For all of its worldly treasures, Italy is perhaps most renowned for its exquisite and simple cuisine. The land that spawned Etruscan civilization, the Roman Empire, and the Renaissance is celebrated just as roundly for *gnocchi di patate*, *ravioli verdi*, and *risotto coi funghi*. It should come as no surprise, then, that the kitchen—the font of these delicacies—is the heart and soul of the Italian household. In the countryside especially, where the pace of the day allows a more subtle appreciation for good food and talk, life revolves around mealtimes and the kitchen and dining room.

Because of the closeness of the Italian family, mealtime is sacred in many households even today. From the morning's espresso to *la pranza*, or lunch, at midday and finally *la cena*, or dinner, families still choose to eat together at the kitchen table whenever possible. And more often than not, meals are taken in leisure, the food and company well savored.

The design of the Italian country kitchen is as simple and timeless as the meals prepared there. White plaster walls, terra-cotta tile floor, exposed beam ceiling—these elements are the foundation of the traditional *cucina rustica*. Like all Italian interiors, the kitchen is kept *ben sistemato*—organized and neat. Surfaces are uncluttered and the overall aspect of the room is spare and minimal.

Although renovated country houses are well accessorized with the latest stovetops and ovens, the massive, smoke-stained hearth or brick oven still conjures images of the Italian mother tending black cauldrons of boiling pasta hanging over the fire. The sink was traditionally made of hand-hewn travertine marble or *pietra serena*, a provincial stone, although more modern enamel sinks are certainly suitable. Local ceramic tiles are often set around the sink area and on countertops, usually in bright, vivid colors that look wonderful against the kitchen's backdrop of earth tones. Wooden cupboards are usually built into the walls to hold dishes and pantry goods.

*La tavola*, or the table, is one of the most essential pieces of furniture in the Italian home. Nothing else epitomizes country living quite like the kitchen table. Italians can spend hours around the table, enjoying a meal with friends and relatives, telling stories, and laughing, above all. The table

OPPOSITE: *In Italy, country charm is all in the details: a wreath of pinecones on the wall and a miniature greenhouse of herbs and spices beside a stoneware* acqua *pitcher on the windowsill. Bentwood chairs and hand-painted wall tiles complete the setting.*

is typically long and rectangular, made of heavy, coarse pine or chestnut. The top is well-worn and smooth, with nicks and scratches only adding to its charm. Chairs are simple in design, with slightly frayed rush seats giving a lived-in look.

Another traditional kitchen furnishing is the *madia*, a small cabinet table that once served as a bread cupboard. Today it is typically used as portable counter space, as useful for holding a microwave oven as it is for storing bread. A painted wood credenza can be used to display collections of local arts and crafts. The artisan tradition is still very much alive in the Italian countryside, with regional specialties ranging from majolica and pewter to glassware and pottery. A carved wood cassone, or chest can be used to store linens.

Hanging on walls or over the hearth, gleaming copper pots and pans bring unusual geometry and warm color to the kitchen environment. In keeping with the rigorous sense of organization, other cooking implements are readily available at arm's reach. What really makes the Italian country kitchen transcendent is the abundance of fresh produce, especially in the summer months. Rosemary and basil plants growing in terra-cotta pots and hanging baskets or wooden bowls filled with fruits and vegetables give a sense of bounteous country living.

In the dining room, setting the table is an art form in itself. Again, simple elegance is the key, even for casual dining. A crisp white tablecloth is the foundation of the well-dressed table. Italy is renowned for its sumptuous linens which are impeccably woven and embroidered with only the most subtle of patterns and motifs.

Place settings are refined yet understated. Simple white porcelain is appropriate for just about any occasion, but hand-painted ceramics lend a country flavor to more informal affairs. Clear crystal stemware and unadorned flatware are country standards. A carafe is used for both wine and water for all but the most casual meals, when the bottles can be placed on the table.

**ABOVE:** *Incredibly, this brilliantly renovated kitchen once served as a cowshed. The conversion left the room wide-open, maximizing the vast sense of space provided by the vaulted ceilings. Uncluttered, smooth surfaces are an Italian trademark—especially in the kitchen, where one finds* tutto a posto, *everything in order.*

ABOVE: *The best dining rooms are comfortable as well as attractive. As many hours are passed at the dining room table, all the senses should be satisfied. Mellow lighting and thin, diaphanous curtains create a cozy and warm ambience. For those fortunate enough to possess a green thumb, an indoor trellis or a few strands of well-trained ivy certainly imbue a rustic quality.*

OPPOSITE: *Floral motifs go a long way in a country decor. Here, small delicate roses decorate the china, which harmonizes perfectly with both the curtains and the glazed wall sconces—splendid bouquets of spring flowers. As a final touch, fresh flowers adorn the table.*

caffè
tè

**OPPOSITE:** *In northern Alpine regions, interiors are commonly paneled in wood. From floor to ceiling, every square inch of this kitchen seems to be covered in lovely blond pine. The room's warm, supple glow is augmented by shiny copper pots and pans hanging on the walls.*

**RIGHT:** *Italian kitchens cannot be outdone for their economy of space. This renovated kitchen benefits from a high ceiling that allows a sleek row of shelves to display peculiar cooking implements. The striated wood floor and cabinets bring unusual texture to the room.*

ABOVE: *Flowing folds of gauze make wonderful drapery in a sunroom. The quality of light is enhanced, and the room takes on an ethereal quality. A wisteria-covered, trompe l'oeil trellis around the entrance blends nicely with real ivy creeping up the walls. In a room so minimally decorated, each detail assumes heightened significance: the table setting is impeccable and the terra-cotta-tiled floor exudes a warm glow.*

OPPOSITE: *This dining room has an unmistakably English flavor. The blue and white checked tablecloth and upholstery make dining indoors feel rather like a picnic. That, of course, is the idea of a country retreat. The china and glassware impeccably complement the color theme.*

**RIGHT:** *Lighting plays an important role in every interior. Here, especially, the lighting has a vital effect on the ambience. The wall sconces radiate a soft light that captures the subtle nuances of the lime-painted walls. Too much light would wash out the color entirely. As it is, the room has a warm, intimate glow.*

**BELOW:** *Rural decors can be quite modern without sacrificing the simplicity of country living. Although the furniture in this dining area is contemporary in design, it is similar to more traditional country pieces in its heavy, spare construction and minimal decoration.*

ABOVE: *The generous proportions and unusual architecture of many farmhouses allow for quite extraordinary conversions. The ground floor—commonly animal stables in traditional* case coloniche*—is where contemporary renovators give their imaginations free reign. Vaulted ceilings often provide a majestic dining room setting. Large barn doors are usually replaced by delicate windows or French doors leading to a terrace garden.*

ABOVE: *Original architectural details bring a sense of history to many renovated country retreats. Here, a massive, nineteenth-century olive press occupies the corner of a dining room, remembering the days when the farm produced olive oil. Such an unusual piece of machinery makes the room truly unique. Of course, the other furnishings are remarkable as well—particularly the beautiful Persian rugs, antique leather chairs, and marble table.*

**OPPOSITE:** *Even in modern country decors, the integrity and nobleness of building materials are apparent. Walls are covered in thick plaster and given a subtle lime wash of color. Balustrades and window grilles are cast in sturdy wrought iron, and delicate French doors open onto a brick terrace.*

**RIGHT, TOP:** *A glass-enclosed breakfast room is a perfect addition to a country retreat. Life in the countryside is all about communing with nature, and what better way than to take the morning's espresso surrounded by lush greenery.*

**RIGHT, BOTTOM:** *Nothing symbolizes Italian country living quite like the kitchen table. It is here where family and friends convene several times a day to enjoy each other's company over a good meal. The table is generally made of heavy, knotted, thick-cut wood. The smooth, polished surface shows the hieroglyphic stains and scratches of countless gatherings.*

**LEFT:** *Often hundreds of years old and typically made of carved marble or stone, a splendid old fireplace is the focus of many country dining rooms. In northern regions, ornate wood mantelpieces are also quite common. This rather formal eighteenth-century mantel is well appointed, topped by an antique mirror and flanked by baroque wall sconces.*

**OPPOSITE:** *Since the dawn of the Renaissance, trompe l'oeil decorative techniques have been employed in homes throughout the Italian countryside. Classical architectural motifs such as columns, pilasters, cornices, and pediments are commonly featured. Ornate wainscoting and floral boughs embellish the walls of this dining room, giving the space architectural definition. The room's classical furnishings enhance the illusion of being in an ancient Roman salon.*

**RIGHT:** *Some of the most beautiful aspects of Italian country architecture can be appreciated only from the inside. Massive roof supports line the ceiling of this second-floor kitchen, giving the room an interesting linear configuration. A skylight provides warm lighting and opens up the space.*

**BELOW:** *Even informal table settings feel special in the cozy confines of an Italian kitchen. Red and white gingham fabric is a country standard, and a deeply polished table certainly enhances the dining experience.*

**OPPOSITE:** *The flavor of Italian country living comes through in this rustic dining room with its exposed wood beam ceilings, walls lined with fine wines, linen tablecloth, and decorative place settings.*

LEFT: *This Alpine kitchen impresses with its rustic simplicity and rich textures. The architecture is remarkably sturdy, fortified with dark hardwood floors, heavy ceiling beams, and walls covered with coarse plaster. The massive, rough-hewn furniture complements the room perfectly. Although modern conveniences like a stove and radiator have been added, the original oven remains, its doors painted an enchanting red.*

ABOVE: *Rustic indeed, this dining room seems like a hollow in the earth's crust. The bare stone walls have a cavernous quality that is nevertheless made to feel quite cozy. The wall sconces have a chiaroscuro effect on the rough surfaces and cast a warm glow across the deeply polished ceiling. A finely embroidered white tablecloth brightens the setting as well. Slender, wrought-iron chairs complete the scene.*

OPPOSITE: *A pantry off the kitchen can be used to store produce and is often quite picturesque in its own right. A bounty of fresh fruits and vegetables hanging from the rafters or filling a marble basin captures the essence of country living. The rough-hewn modesty of the pantry is perhaps its most poignant quality.*

CHAPTER THREE

# LIVING SPACES

Italians are a loquacious people. They enjoy good, spirited conversation. A lazy country afternoon is occasion enough to celebrate with hours of laughing and talking. In cool months these hours are passed *nel salotto*, in the living room, but whenever possible Italians like to be outside on a terrace or under a portico.

Inside and out, living spaces are remarkable for their simple elegance. In the *salotto* furniture is generally placed around the edge of the room. This arrangement creates a feeling of space and order, but can also imbue a rather formal air. However formal the living room may appear, it is certainly never fussy or stiff. A few well-chosen pieces of furniture, often rough-hewn and heavyset, are positioned to bring out the beauty of the architectural elements. The living room, which is often a converted cowshed, may have a vaulted brick ceiling that gives the room a lofty and especially grand appearance. A rosy terra-cotta floor and softly hued stucco walls lend great warmth and texture to the room. The mantel over the fireplace, while ornately carved, displays only a single vase of flowers or a few collected objects. French doors leading out to the terrace garden are graceful, the windows bare or dressed in light, diaphanous folds. In every detail, restraint is employed to create an elegant, yet comfortable ambience.

A balance is achieved between "authentic" country furnishings and more modern, comfortable pieces. A comfortable couch or two is usually the

OPPOSITE: *Italian villas can be quite stately without undermining the charm of country living. This villa has the architectural trappings of a grand palazzo, yet the furnishings are simple and unpretentious, creating an atmosphere that is both relaxed and hospitable. Lighting plays a key role here, as thin drapes open up the space and provide panoramic views of the countryside.*

BELOW: *Curious antiques can be found throughout the Italian countryside. This rococo settee has a mellow, distressed finish that melds with the surroundings perfectly.*

centerpiece of the room. Upholstered in sturdy fabric with soft earth tones or muted floral prints, these are arranged to create a feeling of comfort and intimacy. After all, family and friends can spend hours here chatting. Although the coffee table is a relatively modern invention, it is nevertheless found in many country retreats. A small carved *cassone*, or chest, will often do the trick, or a column pedestal or cornice can be given a glass top and used as a coffee table.

A few pieces of *mobili rustici*, or rustic furniture, go a long way toward creating a country look. Antique country furnishings were simply designed and often homemade, lending them an *arte povera* quality that has only recently become fashionable. Without much demand, the majority of country furniture has been discarded over time and is, therefore, often hard to find. For a price, of course, wonderful pieces from as early as the eighteenth century can still be bought in local shops.

The traditional Florentine table, with its ornamented hexagonal or octagonal top and carved pedestal, can be used alongside a couch or group of chairs. A *cassapanca*, which is a large chest with arms and a back, is a traditional, if not very comfortable, settee. Other Italian classics recognized more for old-world charm than comfort are folding, X-shaped Savonarola and Dante armchairs or pious *sgabello* sidechairs, all of which can be made more hospitable with a plush seat cushion.

All sense of formality is lost when the party moves outdoors. During the summer months, outdoor space is annexed as an extra room or wing of the house. No country home is complete without a portico or a pergola covered in wisteria vines leading out to the gardens. Here, the family and friends can convene in the cool shade even when the midday sun is at its peak. Often second-story bedrooms will have their own *loggie*, or covered balconies, as well.

Italian outdoor retreats meld seamlessly into nature. Stone walls reflect the mellow colors and rich texture of the surrounding landscape, as do the lichen-covered *coppi* tiles on the roof. The use of terra-cotta is nowhere more poignant than here. Patios are often lined with mossy, loosely fitted terra-cotta tiles. Terra-cotta pots and urns are everywhere, overflowing with geraniums and ivy. Stair railings

and gates are wrought iron, which weathers well, and stone balustrades are common around more stately terraces.

Dining alfresco in the countryside is any Italophile's dream come true. Many porticoes and pergolas are large enough for a long dining table, which can be anything from a simple picnic table to a more elaborate lacquered banquet. It is not uncommon for a wrought-iron table to be placed right in the garden, shaded by trees or a beautiful canvas umbrella.

ABOVE: *An open hearth provides ample heat and a lovely setting for an Alpine living room. The hooded wood mantelpiece is several centuries old. To the left of the fireplace is a lovely folk artwork painted on a wooden board. Baskets of dried flowers make attractive country decorations.*

**OPPOSITE:** *To insulate from both summer heat and winter cold, farmhouse walls were often made two feet (61cm) thick. Window openings were quite small and few and far between. A late Renaissance chestnut chair and desk perfectly complement this setting.*

**RIGHT:** *Elaborate frescoes cover the walls of many country villas outside Venice, as gifted artists could often be lured away from the city to embellish country retreats. This splendid landscape is a contemporary rendering, but certainly captures the flavor of the Renaissance. An antique birdcage adds a Victorian touch. Painted chairs hail from the eighteenth century, when Venetian artists began imitating Eastern lacquering techniques.*

ABOVE: *The symmetry of the architecture and the furnishings—not to mention the Roman bust framed against the back arch—lend this lavish portico a formal, classical air. A host of comfortable, broad-striped lounge chairs alleviates any feeling of stuffiness, and gives the space a charming appeal.*

OPPOSITE: *Authentic country antiques are hard to come by in Italy, but a few winning pieces can make a room. A chestnut trestle table is as sturdy and functional today as it was a century ago. A* sgabello *chair, on the other hand, is a precious find, but probably best admired from afar.*

ABOVE: *Leather-backed Dante chairs and a large antique credenza complement a carved limestone fireplace in this well-appointed living room. A collection of ancient busts and other artifacts is displayed on the mantel. In the back of the room two stone pedestals support a glass table top.*

LEFT: *Glazed terra-cotta is a centuries-old Italian tradition. Luca della Robbia glorified the art form in the fifteenth century, but by and large the practice has remained the domain of country artisans. Like all Italian folk art, glazed terra-cotta has a vast iconography and countless regional nuances. A favored medium of the* arte povera *tradition, terra-cotta crafts often have religious or allegorical themes.*

OPPOSITE: *Terra-cotta, stone, wood, and plaster are the basic ingredients of all traditional Italian homes. Country houses look and feel like fortresses because of the integrity and strength of these bulking materials, which are seldom hidden from view.* Pietra serena, *a dense, rich stone common throughout Italy, outlines the portals of this living room.*

PRÈS LE SKI
RESTAURANTS TYPIQUES

**ABOVE:** *Garden furniture like this canvas reclining chair is often used indoors to create a casual look. Wooden marionettes and other folk sculptures are fun country decorations that add to the relaxed, unpretentious atmosphere. If a room is small in size, mirrors and white upholstered furnishings can be used to give the illusion of space. Trees and plants are always welcome additions to a country living room.*

**LEFT:** *Small living spaces rarely seem cramped in the country. Most are instead made to feel quite intimate and cozy. A few comfortable chairs and couches around the fireplace will usually suffice, as in this rustic northern living room.*

ABOVE: *A makeshift portico has a rustic quality and can be made out of just about anything. To open up the house, this portico was added by using granite pillars to hold up a simple wood canopy. Furnished with simple wrought-iron lawn furniture painted a vivid blue, the portico looks charming and—more importantly—provides a comfortable outdoor space.*

OPPOSITE: *With only a green carpet of lawn separating it from the ocean, this pergola offers cool shade and a wonderful view. The columns have been trained with flowering vines that have climbed to the canopy, which is lined with bamboo reeds. The colorful, inlaid-tile table and wicker chairs complete this summery setting.*

**OPPOSITE:** *Even in the mountains it gets pretty warm in the summertime, and Italians like nothing more than retreating to the pergola for lunch. Outdoor wooden furniture weathers quickly here and takes on a nice patina. Simple chairs with rush seats look charming in just about any country setting, indoors or out.*

**RIGHT:** *A terrace garden is the perfect place to set even the most formal table. A little shade is nice, of course, so pick a spot at least partially covered by a tree.*

**ABOVE:** *The portico of this renovated farmhouse is remarkable for its muscular architecture. The integrity of the construction—the fine masonry and brickwork—imbues the space with a stalwart character. The simple architecture can afford tasteful, modern lighting fixtures. Terra-cotta planters accent the building's earth tones.*

ABOVE: *Lichen-covered stone walls have a special poignancy in the Italian countryside. They often seem to be as timeless and stoic as the land itself. This wall fronts a stately Tuscan villa.*

**LEFT:** *Ivy trims the entire length of this Alpine house and gives this portico a rustic countenance. White-washed walls and green shutters complement these ivy "whiskers" nicely, while red plaid curtains in the kitchen look picture-perfect next to bunches of impatiens.*

**LEFT:** *Artfully stenciled walls give this spectacular view a run for its money. Subtle pastels give the interior a warm glow, while large windows usher in the countryside's natural beauty. With views like these, a room needs little else to be fully furnished.*

**BELOW:** *A brace of delicate French doors opens off this grand rotunda, bringing the countryside right into the living room. The inlaid floor and classical wall moldings complement both the shape and proportions of the room. Plump couches make this formal setting quite comfortable and welcoming.*

**RIGHT:** *Capri's sprawling downtown makes an interesting mosaic from a neighboring hillside pergola. The dappled shade of the vine-covered trellis is a nice place to take in the view and enjoy dining alfresco. Fanciful wrought-iron chairs seem to imitate the tendrils creeping along the pergola.*

**BELOW:** *Color is an important element in outdoor table setting. The colors of the natural landscape seem to have an especially buoyant effect on the Italian table. Here, navy-rimmed china and a sky blue tablecloth are accented by yellow-cushioned chairs and red flowers placed at each setting.*

ABOVE: *Large, glassed-in archways make this living room a country paradise. Indeed, when sitting on one of the plush couches, one has the feeling of being outdoors. With ivy trained along the arches inside, the window panes do not seem to stem the encroaching wilderness. The room's subtle white and cream palette is cool and serene.*

**ABOVE:** *The quality of light at dusk can be quite evocative throughout the Italian countryside. This partially covered loggia offers a great view of an especially surreal twilight. The architecture is simple and seems to acquiesce to the profound beauty of the landscape. The massive walls emphasize the lyric quality of the slender wrought-iron chairs.*

**OPPOSITE:** *The Italian coastline offers many spectacular vistas, but none more stunning than the one from this cliff-top portico. The structure provides shelter from the sun without taking away from the view. The horizontal, clean lines of the architecture are mirrored by those of the furniture, which is simple and solidly built.*

CHAPTER FOUR

# BED AND BATH

Life in the Italian countryside is all about enjoying time spent with family and friends. The intimacies of the kitchen and living rooms and the beautiful vastness of the outdoors set the stage for relaxed, lazy days and nights passed eating and drinking, talking and socializing. Life is very much removed from the pressures of the modern world, and country dwellers appreciate the chance to visit and be together.

The bedroom, therefore, is not the prime focus of the country retreat, as the sparseness of the decor may suggest. In the Italian countryside, the bedroom is basically just that—a room with a bed—and it is used primarily for sleeping. Here, especially, a few finely made pieces of furniture suffice. The bedroom is generally not a nest feathered for private escape, for the attraction of the country home lies elsewhere.

Which is not to say the bedroom isn't quaint and comfortable—it is both. The sense of uncluttered space is a luxury in itself. The openness allows the architecture of the room to feature prominently. Often the roofline and exposed rafters create an unusual canopy. The ceiling and beams are traditionally whitewashed with lime. Walls are painted off-white or another warm, muted color. The floors are dark stained wood or worn stone and are rarely carpeted. A few throw rugs can soften the effect of the bare floors without taking away from the clean lines of the space.

The single most prominent piece of furniture is, of course, the bed. In the master bedroom, the *letto matrimoniale*, or matrimonial bed, has an elaborate headbord usually made of carved wood or sculpted iron. In stately country villas, these are often quite fancy displays of craftsmanship, the wood carved and gilded in magnificent relief.

The *baldacchino*, or canopy bed, is still popular in rural settings, if for no other reason than to protect the sleeper from flaking whitewash. But they are beautiful too. The Tyrolean bed, with its heavy, carved, painted wooden canopy, is a magnificent find in many villas in the northern Alps. These enormous beds can afford rich velvet or brocaded drapes—the better for keeping warm in the winter months. In Tuscany and Umbria, baldachins are usually cast in slender wrought iron, which can be lyrically embellished but which is more often crafted in sleek rectilinear forms. These canopies are left bare or are draped in lightweight linens with a soft, neutral color. Either way, the clean lines of the bed are

OPPOSITE: *Although the process of stenciling the plaster walls of this bedroom was complex and labor-intensive, the finished effect is astonishing. Furnishings are few, enhancing the setting by not taking away from the ornate wall design.*

preserved. Further south, Spanish influence is evident in the ornately carved and turned four-poster beds, which are distinguished by their spiraling balustrades. According to Italian tradition, a religious painting or symbol crowned with a small olive branch hangs over most beds to protect the sleeper.

Bed linens, like table linens, are possessions worthy of investment. Italy is home to some of the world's most famous linen manufacturers, and quality bedding is a mark of distinction. In the country, bed linens are notable not only for their exceptional quality, but also for their simple design and subtle texture. Dust ruffles and frilly shams and bedcovers do not appeal to the Italian sense of line and space.

Other bedroom furnishings are few. Massive wood *armadi*, or wardrobes, are great for storing clothes. They are plainly carved and often decorated with nail studs or other simple hardware. In the northern regions, commodes and wardrobes are often lacquered and painted in floral or narrative motifs of the *arte povera* tradition. Italians are famous for the organization of their closet space, so what can't be stored in the *armadio* will most likely be secreted away behind closed doors. A *cassone*, or large chest, can be found in just about any room in an Italian farmhouse, but it is especially useful in the bedroom for storing bed linens or blankets.

Italian country villas and farmhouses are not famous for their plumbing. Until recently, it was not unusual to find *case coloniche* without running water, and what we consider standard bathroom fixtures today were not so standard in the Italian countryside a short time ago. Not surprisingly, therefore, bathrooms in converted farmhouses and restored villas are usually rather modern.

The best way to maintain traditional country decor in the bathroom is by using traditional country materials. As in every other room of the house, terra-cotta tiles or hardwood can be used with great effect on bathroom floors and walls. Locally crafted ceramic tiles bring regional flavor—as well as color—to shower and washbasin areas. Details such as a hand-forged iron towel bar or an original stone or marble sink can make all the difference.

ABOVE: *Many Alpine bedrooms are endowed with enormous hooded hearths. Graced with such a prominent architectural element, the bedroom does not require much decoration. Bare plaster walls impart a great sense of texture, and a few Persian rugs can soften the effect of hardwood floors. Shutters inside and out preclude the need for curtains.*

**LEFT:** *A room with a view is a rare luxury, yet this room has a superb vista. The loggia of the upstairs bedroom is covered with a bamboo lattice. Downstairs, sliding shutter doors open onto a tiled terrace garden. With such inspiring views, the bedroom decor can well afford simplicity. A sumptuous settee completes the setting.*

ABOVE: *Hanging on an Alpine bedroom wall, tyke-size ski poles and skis make a quaint allusion to halcyon days of youth. A few well-chosen furnishings coordinating with the dark exposed wood ceiling beams give a rustic touch to the spare decor.*

ABOVE: *A massive, ornately carved antique crib is the centerpiece of this nursery. With such a singular furnishing, all that's needed to complete the room are a few finely crafted wood toys. The design is spare and sophisticated, but it is also imbued with enough fantasy to inspire any child's imagination.*

OPPOSITE: *High-pitched roofs often make for interesting interior spaces. Ceiling beams jut into this bedroom at wild angles, creating dramatic volumes. These sloped wood ceilings are beautiful not only for their rich, grainy texture, but also for their simple, purposeful construction.*

RIGHT: *If all bedrooms opened onto balconies overlooking the Italian countryside, decorating would be easy. Floral-print curtains and delicate French doors frame this room's lush vista. The walls and bedcovers are finely textured but plainly decorated, designed not to detract from the room's natural beauty.*

LEFT: *From botanical prints on the walls to floral-patterned bedcovers and drapes, a country bedroom looks perfectly quaint outfitted in bright colorful flowers. Coordinating these colors—from lamp shades to ceiling beams—gives the room a finished look. Lyrically embellished wrought-iron beds have an organic quality that follows the theme.*

OPPOSITE: *Country artisans are well trained in the art of trompe l'oeil embellishment. Hanging flower garlands and sprightly vines are painted on the walls and ceiling of this bedroom in Tuscany. The brass beds accent the gold tassels painted on the walls. Although the window is small and narrow, the long, broad curtains make it seem larger.*

ABOVE: *Nothing imparts rustic charm to a bedroom like a hand-patched quilt. Throw one on a bed and the room is immediately transformed. This bedroom happens to be well rusticated already, outfitted as it is with red gingham-covered footstools and side tables. Short candlestick lamps bring diminutive cuteness to the setting, as do miniature botanical prints. The eighteenth-century bed is opulently carved, the headboard inlaid with a glazed ceramic portrait of the Virgin Mary.*

OPPOSITE: *In the country bathroom, a single antique can make the entire room wash. This combination mirror and toiletry drawer is just such a piece. Functional and attractive, its scalloped edges and decorative palings and finials bring a new dimension to the room's straight lines and flat surfaces.*

**LEFT, TOP:** *Straight lines and smooth surfaces are the cornerstones of Italian design, and the bathroom is where these attributes are most apparent. Strong lighting is essential, and quality fixtures—chrome faucets, for example—can greatly enhance the bathroom decor. Lyric embellishments like a wrought-iron hat rack and a carved wooden screen complement the rigid linearity of the bathroom.*

**LEFT, BOTTOM:** *In the Italian Alps, diamond-shaped window mullions are commonly used and suggest an Austrian influence. As elsewhere throughout the Italian countryside, the palette here is subdued and earthy. Woodwork is generally dark, and terra-cotta floors and plaster walls are favored. A white-on-white embroidered bedspread and cream-colored canopy and curtains highlight the texture of the architectural elements.*

**OPPOSITE:** *Thatch roofs are uncommon in Italy, but this renovated farmhouse is none the worse for wear. Wrought-iron beds are a staple throughout the central region, and many antiques are fancifully embellished. Italian appreciation for clean lines and uncluttered space prompts bedcovers to be neatly tucked under the mattress.*

LEFT: *Bedroom furnishings are often the most rustic of all household belongings. Ponderous, knotted-wood beds and a peg-leg stool are classic country fare. They seem wellsuited to a room with split and splintered roof beams. A vase of fresh cut flowers makes a weekend sojourn in the country special.*

OPPOSITE: *With a terrace garden and lofty courtyard view, this villa bedroom is splendidly decadent. Hand-painted French doors lead to a balcony with Gothic carved-stone balustrades. One can almost feel the gentle breeze wafting the smell of gardenias through lustrous folds of damask.*

RIGHT: *Italians are renowned for systematic, orderly interiors, and the bathroom is no exception. The Italian bathroom, in fact, sets the standard for spatial economy. The well-appointed washroom has myriad shelves, drawers, and cabinets. Rustic charm, however, is not lost in the woodwork.*

## INDEX



## PHOTO CREDITS

©Massimo Listri: 22–23, 45, 55, 62, 70, 78

©Alessandra Quaranta: 30–31

Franca Speranza: ©Reto Guntli: 5, 16, 17, 18, 73; ©Simon McBride: 24 left, 63, 75 bottom, 82–83, 88 top; ©Nider: 41, 49, 56, 57, 75 top, 80; ©Marina Papa: 21 right, 65;© Paolo Sacco: 74

© Tim Street-Porter: 61, 95 (designed by Annie Kelly)

©Studio Giancarlo Gardin: 7, 11, 12, 13, 24–25, 30 left, 32, 34–35, 36, 37, 38, 39, 42 left, 42–43, 44, 46, 47 both, 50, 51 both, 52–53, 54, 58–59, 60, 64 top, 66–67, 68, 69, 71, 79, 84, 85, 86, 87, 88 bottom, 89, 90, 91, 92 both, 93, 94 both

©Angelo Tondini/Focus Team: 2, 8, 14, 17, 19 both, 22 left, 26 both, 27, 28 both, 29 both, 40, 48, 64 bottom, 67 right, 72, 76 both, 77

©Steve Vidler/Leo de Wys: 20–21